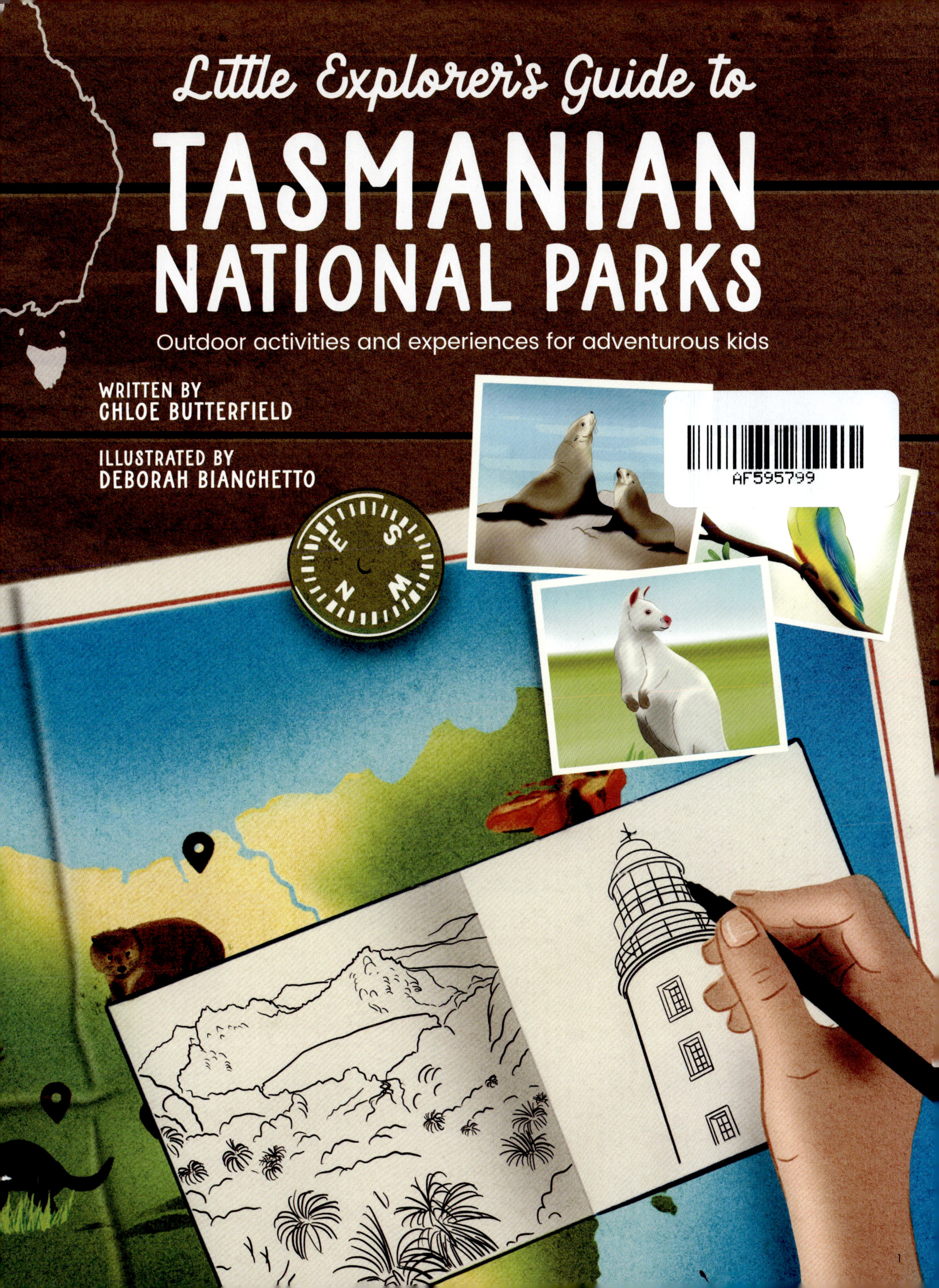
Little Explorer's Guide to
TASMANIAN NATIONAL PARKS
Outdoor activities and experiences for adventurous kids
WRITTEN BY
CHLOE BUTTERFIELD
ILLUSTRATED BY
DEBORAH BIANCHETTO
AF595799

TABLE OF CONTENTS

Launceston

Hobart

NARAWNTAPU
NATIONAL PARK

Sitting right on the boundary of the treacherous Bass Strait, this watery wonderland is home to an incredible amount of wildlife that meanders about.

Which will be your favourite experience? Gazing at the giant expanses of grassland stretching out to the ocean? Admiring the way the light shimmers on the water at dusk? Or perhaps listening to the wild sounds of Tasmanian Devils growling in the depths of night?

NARAWNTAPU NATIONAL PARK

ID CARD

PARK ESTABLISHED: 1976
KNOWN FOR: ENDLESS WATERWAYS AND AQUATIC ANIMALS
SIZE: 44KM^2
HOME OF: PIRINILAPLU PEOPLE
GEOGRAPHY: STUNNING BEACHES AND TINY ISLANDS CELEBRATE THE MIXING OF SALTWATER WITH FRESHWATER

VELVET BUSH

Teeny tiny star-shaped hairs make the leaves of this spreading beauty look a bit like velvet. Grey on top and rusty orange underneath, these cool plants can be found in dry, rocky places. Take it slow and get down low to see their miniature white flowers arranged in star-shaped bunches.

TASMANIAN LONG-EARED BAT

These bats huddle, tucked away in the safety of tree hollows, munching away on insects that don't fly. Their huge ears look almost half as big as their bodies. They use **echolocation** to navigate in the dark – they make a sound, the sound hits an object and they listen to it as it bounces back to them (like an echo). This helps them to tell how far away things are and which materials those things are made of. Watch out for baby bats hitching a ride with their mums – they use special teeth that bend backwards to grab hold.

WHITE-LIPPED SNAKE

These lovely reptiles are named after the white stripe that lashes across their face, marking where their lips would be (if they had any). They're nicely adapted to the cool weather here because they're small, so can heat up faster than big snakes, while their eggs don't need to be kept warm because they don't lay any!

TASMANIAN SMELT

Tiny, shiny, skinny and smelling like cucumber when pulled out of the water – how strange! You can find these little guys where the water flows slowly. Watch as they munch on the larvae of aquatic insects. In spring and summer the parents lay their eggs in the rivers; once they hatch, the babies are swept out to sea to grow before the cycle begins again. Smelt make tasty snacks for platypus, and water rats too.

LONG-NOSED POTOROO

Pottering along, night after night, potoroos help to grow our forests by feeding on fungi and spreading **spores** in their **scats**. The spores grow into new fungi, which help trees to take up more water and nutrients so they can grow tall. The plants thank the potoroos by providing safe homes for them to shelter in and fallen leaves that they use for restful daytime naps. Look near stringybark trees and wet areas for small holes in the ground – evidence of potoroo pottering.

WHITE-FOOTED DUNNART

Weighing in at just a little more than a Tim Tam, these tiny fellows pitter-patter through the bush with white furry feet, big black eyes, piercing needle-like teeth and a sweet little face that looks like a fox! Can you believe that they only breed once in their lives? As the weather moves from winter to spring, the babies are born in a little bark nest hidden under a fallen tree, among rocks, or even in the skirt of a grass tree.

COAST WATTLE

Coast Wattles are excellent habitat for lots of animals here and their strong roots are great for holding soil together and preventing **erosion**. Did you know that the first Australians traditionally ate the gum that seeps from the branches and drank the freshwater stored in their roots? What amazing bush tucker!

FORESTER KANGAROO

The second-largest **marsupial** in the world can stand up to 2 metres tall. These special Tassie friends are very closely related to the Grey Kangaroos you see on the mainland, but have slightly different DNA. Listen carefully because Foresters chat to each other using clucking sounds, and if surprised they might even make a sound like a cough! At dawn and dusk you can catch them munching on succulent grass in open areas.

ACTIVITIES

WORD SEARCH

Learn more about furry creatures of the night by finding all the Potoroo words!

FUNGI
SPORES
SCATS
POTOROO
SHELTER
STRINGYBARK
HOLES
MARSUPIAL
HOP
HABITAT

J	G	A	P	Z	B	H	S	M	S	L	I	H	Y	L	N	Q	J
F	U	N	G	I	R	K	K	P	A	C	D	C	O	I	Z	T	Q
B	M	T	M	H	O	P	U	D	O	R	A	S	H	L	V	G	Q
M	S	H	E	L	T	E	R	J	Y	R	S	T	T	V	E	X	P
V	R	K	U	S	H	X	Y	H	D	B	E	U	S	Z	A	S	U
P	O	T	O	R	O	O	M	E	H	R	A	S	P	P	Z	P	M
I	G	S	T	R	I	N	G	Y	B	A	R	K	P	I	A	U	E
W	O	A	U	B	U	L	T	M	R	H	W	W	N	C	A	Q	M
M	F	V	Z	S	Q	V	F	V	S	J	N	A	I	K	B	L	J
X	C	F	A	K	V	D	S	I	T	P	K	Q	P	F	Z	W	N
Q	H	Q	F	F	I	J	H	R	E	V	B	N	N	X	J	L	A
H	U	M	A	Z	X	H	A	B	I	T	A	T	L	T	P	D	T

SYMMETRY SKETCH

Oh no! The ranger forgot to finish her drawing of the Forester Kangaroo. Use the grid to help you copy the second half.

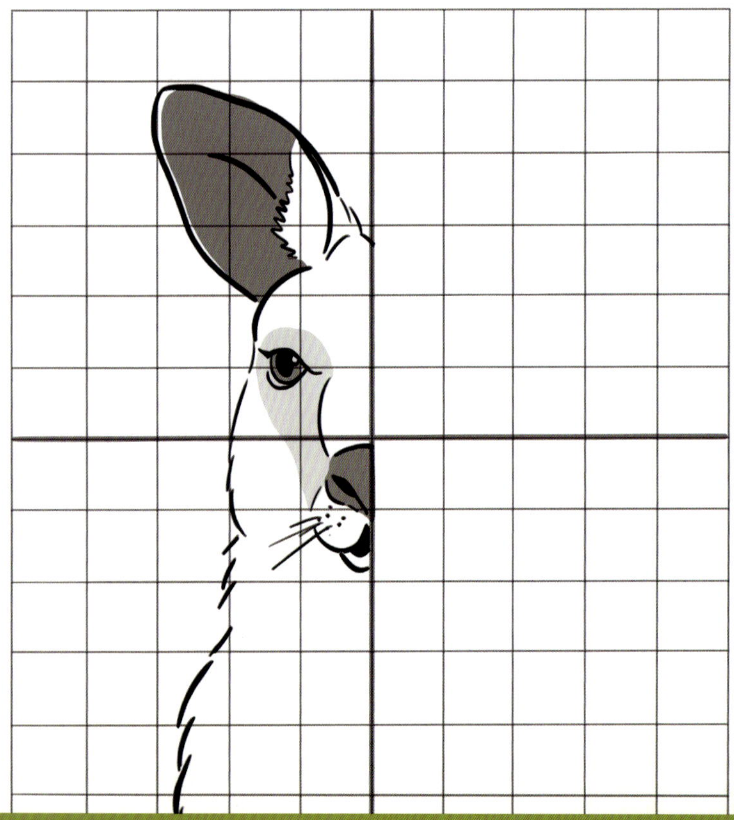

RANGER'S TIP

Humans who collect timber for firewood often disturb potoroo nests, so make sure to check the fire rules in the park first and bring your own fuel during the permitted fire season.

"My favourite thing about my job is the diversity that the work offers. One day I could be firefighting in a remote part of the Tasmanian wilderness, while the next I might be saving dolphins along our beaches, cleaning the amenities or exchanging information with our visitors."

Ranger Jenna

MY MAP

IN YOUR NOTEBOOK, DRAW A MAP OF WHERE YOU'VE BEEN TODAY. USE SYMBOLS AND LABELS FOR LANDMARKS.

MOUNT WILLIAM
NATIONAL PARK

Along this windy coastline where spring flowers bloom, venture over the granite rocks that break down over thousands of years to make the pure white sand of this beautiful place. More than just an incredible view, this park is also packed full of preserved history and bush tucker. Selfies with the bright blue water are a must.

MOUNT WILLIAM NATIONAL PARK

ID CARD

PARK ESTABLISHED:	1973
KNOWN FOR:	VIVIDLY COLOURED ROCKS, FRIENDLY WILDLIFE AND RELAXING WALKS
SIZE:	114KM^2
HOME OF:	TRUWULWAY PEOPLE
GEOGRAPHY:	SECLUDED ROCKY BEACHES STRETCH OUT TO TOUCH GENTLE WAVES OF SAPPHIRE BLUE

COAST BANKSIA

I wonder how many chattering birds and tiny insects you can find in the banksia bushes? These pretty specimens aren't just great habitat, they also have strong roots to hold soil together and the First Nations people of this country use the flowers to make a sweet drink. Banksia seeds actually live inside the cones and wait for fire to make their escape. The ethylene in the smoke opens the cone so the seeds can fall out... remarkable!

SHY ALBATROSS

Tasmania happens to be the only place in the world where this albatross species breeds. When it's time, mums lay only one egg and have to sit on it for 72 days before hatching. The young albatross matures very slowly and it may be ten years before it gets to lay its own eggs. Their wingspan can measure more than 2.5 metres and their body weighs a whopping 4 kilograms. At sea, they spend almost all their time flying and they will eat anything that looks yummy on the surface of the ocean, sadly including rubbish.

CLUES TO CULTURE

There is so much history to be found here, including more than 90 shell middens. A midden is a special site where cooking and eating happened in the past, and scientists use this information to give them clues about history. Middens are special places for Aboriginal people to connect with their culture and they need to be protected. If you find one, never touch or take anything. Built up in huge mounds over time, as the soil and sand erodes away it reveals more shells, bones and secrets. Scientists use **carbon dating** to find out how old the remains are. We can even use middens to see patterns showing which species were eaten in different periods of time. Animals that used to be common, might not be so common anymore.

YELLOW-THROATED HONEYEATER

Tonk tonk tonk – it's a Yellow-throated Honeyeater picking insects off tree trunks. You might even catch them snapping their bills at other birds who come into their territory. Look for nests close to the ground in trees, logs and grass, and lined with animal fur for comfort and warmth. Sometimes these yellow beauties get tricked when cuckoos lay their own eggs in honeyeater nests and the honeyeater parents end up raising a baby cuckoo instead of their own young. Tricky!

LOVELY LICHEN

Take a moment to stop and behold, for atop the rocks cling bright orange lichen, creating a colourful crust you can spot from a mile away. Did you know there are so many types of lichen that many haven't been discovered yet? Lichen are so tough that they can live on almost any surface – even underwater. Lichen is created when algae and fungi partner up and create food which provides energy to grow. They have so many important jobs in our **ecosystems**, such as holding moisture, creating habitat, holding soil together, providing food for animals, giving minerals back to forests and taking nitrogen out of the air to feed to plants. There's not much they *can't* do.

SOOTY OYSTERCATCHER

Tiptoe, tiptoe, stab! An oystercatcher pierces its **prey** by using its pointy beak like a fork. As black as soot from a chimney, their striking feathers are easy to spot. Sooties won't settle for anything less than an ocean view, never venturing further than 50 metres from the beach. They're so attached to the ocean that they even drink seawater – they have special salt glands next to their eyes that take salt out of their blood and eject it from their bodies. Talk about adaptations!

BENNETT'S WALLABY

You're sure to spot many of these macropod friends during your visit. Bennett's is actually a subspecies of the Red-necked Wallaby. Adults feed in open grassy areas but the babies are 'hidden' in the bushes close by for safety once they're out of the pouch. They can hop, but did you know they can also crawl and swim? Wallabies use stored energy in their legs to keep up the hops – the first hop is the trickiest, then at the end of each bounce the energy stored inside their leg muscles counts towards the next hop, and so on and so on. Lookout for clues such as greenish-yellow **scats**.

EASTERN PYGMY POSSUM

With a tiny pink nose, big pointed ears and soft whiskers, this little fella only weighs up to 40 grams – that's about the same as a slice of bread! These teeny-weeny possums love to eat nectar and pollen, so look out for them near flowering gum trees and plants with flowers that look like brushes.

ACTIVITIES

BIRDY BEHAVIOUR

Set a timer and quietly watch one bird around you. Place a tick or tally mark in the box whenever you catch it displaying a different behaviour. It's amazing what you can learn when you stop to watch.

BEHAVIOUR	NUMBER OF TIMES OBSERVED
PECK	
HOP	
FLY	
LISTEN	
CALL	
EAT	

"My favourite part of my job is meeting a diverse range of people, from interstate visitors to local Tasmanians, who are all enjoying the natural beauty of *Wukalina/* Mount William National Park."
Ranger Nathan

RANGER'S TIP

Help out our garbage-guts albatrosses by trying really hard to use less stuff, make less waste and dispose of rubbish carefully.

MAP MADNESS

Maps are essential for the safe passage of explorers through the bush. Below is a list of which animals live at different locations on the map, can you sketch them in the correct places?

A4 - Bennett's Wallaby
C2 - Coast Banksia
D3 - Eastern Pygmy Possum
B1 - Shy Albatross
E6 - Sooty Oystercatcher

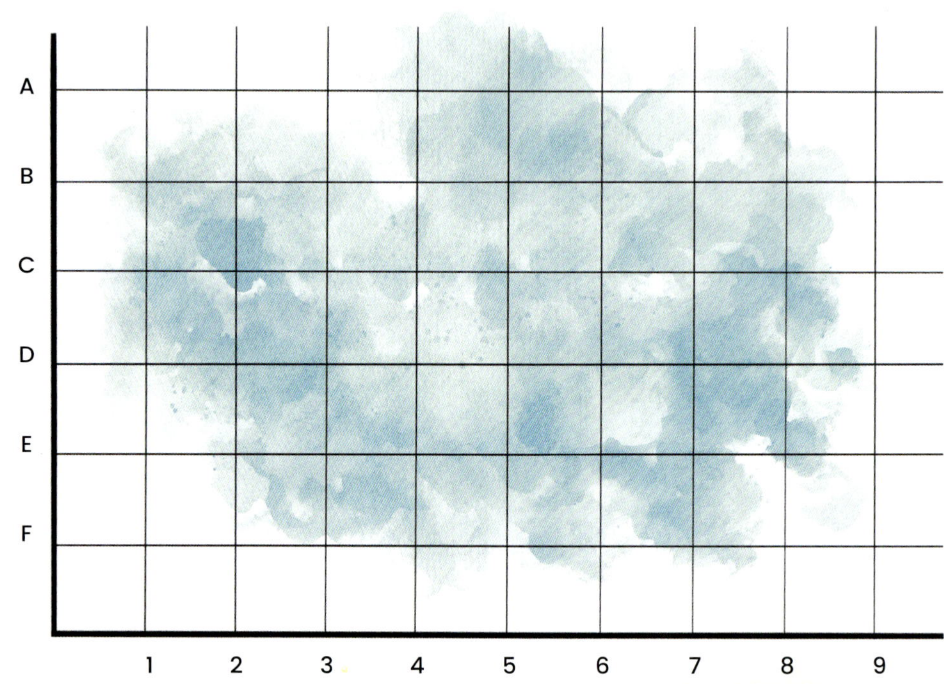

WHO AM I? *IN YOUR NOTEBOOK, WRITE OUT SOME FACTS (CLUES) ABOUT A SECRET ANIMAL FROM THIS CHAPTER OR YOUR TRAVELS AND HAVE YOUR TRAVEL COMPANIONS GUESS WHICH ONE IT IS.*

FREYCINET
NATIONAL PARK

Famous the world over, with water so clear you can watch your feet wriggle, Freycinet is an experience not to be missed. A fabulous explosion of contrasting colours greets you each day – from bright orange rocks to squeaky white sand and sparkling azure seas – along with mountains of granite and caves full of life.

FREYCINET NATIONAL PARK

ID CARD

LITTLE EXPLORER'S GUIDE

PARK ESTABLISHED:	1916
KNOWN FOR:	SWEEPING BAYS AND CRYSTAL-CLEAR WATER
SIZE:	169 KM^2
HOME OF:	TOORERNO-MAIRE-MENER PEOPLE
GEOGRAPHY:	ROCKY BEACHES BELOW GRANITE HILLS

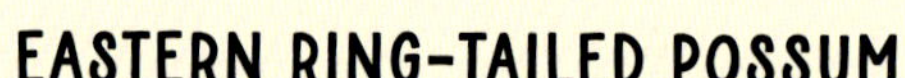

EASTERN RING-TAILED POSSUM

Bang, crash, rustle… these adorable acrobats swing, leap and hang with such skill; using their white-tipped tails as a third hand for grabbing. Mums and dads build special nests called 'dreys' together and the dads are the only male possums known to help the mums by carrying the babies while she eats in peace. To get a second go at the nutrients that already came out the other end, they often eat their own poo!

LITTLE PENGUIN

The little pink feet, blue-black feathers and waddle of the smallest penguin in the world melts hearts year after year. Unlike other penguins, they don't love ice, so hang out here among the rocks and sand. Ever wondered why they waddle? They have little legs but big feet for swimming (like wearing fins for snorkelling). Penguins eat lots of important foods such as fish, squid, krill and **crustaceans**, so any change to penguin numbers gives scientists a clue there might be something wrong in the food chain.

RED-BELLIED PADEMELON

These furry friends have a red-brown tummy, which is how they got their name. They have short little tails so they don't get caught among the branches as they forage for food among dense bushes. Pademelons used to be a favourite food of Thylacines, now they still make an important meal for Tasmanian Devils.

WEDGE-TAILED EAGLE

High in the sky with a long pointed tail, circling in search of lunch, Australia's largest bird of **prey** can be seen, giving a steely stare as it drifts past. These birds are enormous – they can weigh more than 5 kilograms and have a wingspan in excess of 2 metres. Wedge-tails are exceptional hunters because they can actually squeeze and lengthen their eyeballs to zoom their vision, a bit like a camera lens.

PIGFACE

Not your average pink little piggies, this amazing plant loves to live on sand dunes. They're incredibly important for holding dunes together with their roots and also form a special **habitat** for many other species. Their fat triangular leaves hold water and feel squishy to touch. This plant makes excellent bush tucker because the fruit, leaves and even the flowers can be eaten.

SOUTHERN RIGHT WHALE

These whales are big and swim close to the shore, so they were easier to catch during the days of whaling. Because of this, they were known as the 'right' whales to hunt. With their huge, slow bodies, they swim flat along the water, mouths open to let food swim right in. They're missing a **dorsal fin** and instead have two blowholes! Those bumpy bits on their heads are called 'callosities' and these are what scientists use to recognise each whale when they study them – a bit like a fingerprint for humans.

TIGER SNAKE

Thick with a short head and shy; Tiger Snakes don't always have stripes. Depending on where they live, their colour can change from black to grey to sandy or stripy. During winter, they keep warm by sleeping in burrows that other animals have made – and when real estate is at a premium, sometimes 20 or more can be found together! These snakes are very important to **ecosystems** because they eat pests that harm our environment. Even though Tiger Snakes are dangerously **venomous**, they still use constriction (squeezing) before eating their **prey**.

AUSTRALASIAN GANNET

Whooooosh! A gannet falls out of the sky with spectacular drama, plunging into the ocean like a rocket and folding its wings back right before it hits the water. Even though these speedy **predators** only spend ten seconds below, they've already eaten their fish before they resurface. They have special air sacs under their skin that act like mini airbags, so they don't get hurt as they dive hard into the water.

ACTIVITIES

SOOTHING SOUNDS

Take a walk through the bush, listening carefully for even the faintest noise. Use the circle to record with tally marks how many times you count each type of sound. I wonder who's making all that racket?

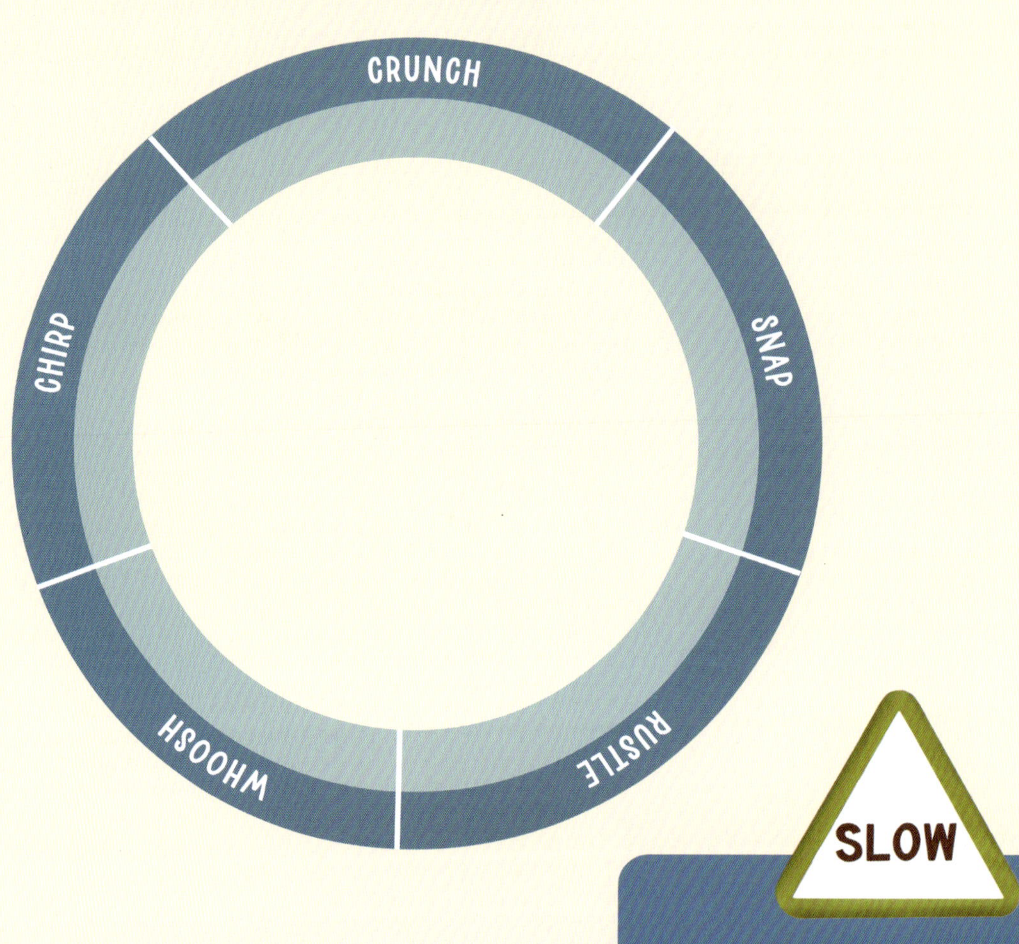

SLOW

RANGER'S TIP

Get down low and go slow, slow, slow for your best chance of a peek at shy mammals like pademelons.

"I feel very lucky to help look after this incredible park for all the visitors to enjoy. I often think I have the best office in the world."
Ranger Marty

A-MAZE-ING

Complete the maze and help Little Penguin find his way back to shore. Be careful you don't bump into anyone along the way!

BIG BURROW ENERGY

IMAGINE YOU'RE A TIGER SNAKE, LOOKING FOR A SAFE PLACE TO REST YOUR WEARY HEAD. IN YOUR NOTEBOOK DESIGN THE COOLEST SNAKE BURROW YOU CAN DREAM UP. I WONDER WHAT YOU'LL USE TO MAKE IT EXTRA COSY?

MARIA ISLAND
NATIONAL PARK

From Maria Island painted cliffs plunge deep into a secret underwater world where giant lobsters creep and kelp forests sway. There's something new to see everyday. Back on land learn about the many things that have happened here in history while you wander among wombats, geese and even more animal friends.

MARIA ISLAND NATIONAL PARK

ID CARD

PARK ESTABLISHED:	1972
KNOWN FOR:	PRISTINE ECOSYSTEMS FULL OF WILDLIFE
SIZE:	96.7KM^2
HOME OF:	PUTHIKWILAYTI PEOPLE OF WUKALUWIKIWYNA (MARIA ISLAND)
GEOGRAPHY:	WHITE SANDY BEACHES STRETCH LONG AGAINST GOLDEN ROCKS AND GENTLE BUSHLAND

EASTERN GREY KANGAROO

Cluck, cluck – a mob of Eastern Greys talk to each other while they forage for grass, plants and fungi. You'll be able to spot this common 'big foot' almost everywhere across the eastern half of Australia. In the cooler parts of the day, or in the evening, they graze on the greenest grass because it contains more nutrients and is extra delicious.

KELP FOREST

No explorers, kelp are NOT plants – the floating green towers you see here are actually giant algae! These amazing organisms can reach up to 40 metres tall and grow up to 50 centimetres in a single day. Unfortunately warming waters are making ocean life difficult, so scientists have been experimenting with how to help our underwater forests. They took spores from kelp that was surviving in warm water, grew them in a lab and took them back to sea. In a year, they grew to 12 metres tall!

Here are five reasons we need to keep our kelp:

1 Kelp forests make amazing habitat
2 Snorkelling is magical here
3 They capture carbon
4 They take pollution out of water
5 Kelp holds cultural value and was traditionally used to carry water

TASMANIAN DUSKY ANTECHINUS

These tiny **carnivores** like to nest alone. They are **diurnal**, so you might catch them sunbaking during the day. There are many different antechinus species across the country and each has its different quirks. Usually crazy dirt diggers, they fossick for insects, worms and spiders using long claws for scratching and long whiskers for sensing.

CAPE BARREN GOOSE

Ark-ark-ark... geese trumpet overhead as they fly in search of open, grassy areas to feed. Pairs mate for life and males build nests on the ground, which they make comfortable by adding tiny fluffy feathers called 'down'. These geese are perfectly adapted to island life because they can drink salty water, which means they can stay on islands without fresh water all year if they need to – how clever!

SOUTHERN ROCK LOBSTER

Growing to a huge weight of 5 kilograms, with eyes on the ends of stalks to see many angles and two spines that look more like horns, these creatures of the deep are fascinating to look at. Lobsters even change colour with depth – they are orange in the shallows and purple-red in the deep. You might catch them crunching on spiky urchins or pushing themselves forward underwater using pairs of 'swimmerets' under their abdomen. Look out for them wedged into small gaps in the reef.

PAINTED CLIFFS

Be prepared to become mesmerised by the swirls of creamy colour in this fantastic rock. Water from the surface filters down through the porous sandstone and stains the rock.

The wind and waves blast away tiny sections of rock and make beautiful shapes and patterns. Check the tide – you want to visit when it's low so you can get down to the bottom safely. Take a snorkel for an extra adventure.

WEEDY SEADRAGON

These dragons of the deep float along on the current, dangling their body parts like seaweed for **camouflage**. At night, the ladies and gentlemen dragons dance to show they like each other, and not long after the eggs are laid. Daddy dragons carry the eggs and can haul up to 250 under their tail.

CUTTLEFISH

These cephalopods are a little bit inside-out, holding their shell, which is called a cuttlebone, inside the body. Sometimes you find cuttlebones washed ashore – birds like to sharpen their beaks on them. Cuttlefish have 10 appendages – eight are arms for swimming, moving and eating, while two are long tentacles that whip out fast to catch **prey** and quickly shove it into their mouth. Cuttlefish have amazing colour-changing abilities; watch as they blend in with the colours of the reef, changing as they move.

ACTIVITIES

PEEKABOO, WHERE ARE YOU?

Can you find all the seadragons and lobsters in the wavy kelp forest?

RANGER'S TIP

Although kangaroos can jump an astonishing 6 metres with a single hop, they are still victims of car accidents, so take care on roads at dawn and dusk.

"If you stay still and quiet and carefully look around, the bush will come to life. You can spot lots of different native animals and birds if you look closely."

Ranger Geoff

CRAZY CROSSWORD

Use the clues to discover the secret words and write them in the boxes on the crossword.

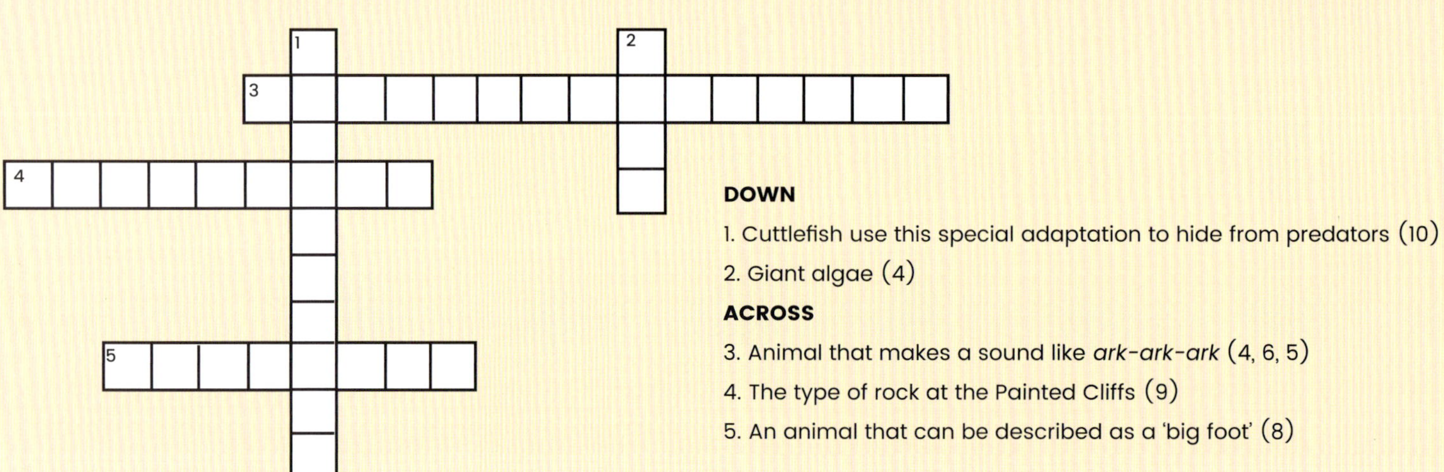

DOWN

1. Cuttlefish use this special adaptation to hide from predators (10)
2. Giant algae (4)

ACROSS

3. Animal that makes a sound like *ark-ark-ark* (4, 6, 5)
4. The type of rock at the Painted Cliffs (9)
5. An animal that can be described as a 'big foot' (8)

SIT SPOT *FIND A COMFY SPOT TO SIT IN NATURE AND SET A TIMER FOR TWO MINUTES. NOTICE ALL THE SIGHTS AND SOUNDS AROUND YOU AND THE FEELINGS INSIDE YOU. SOME PEOPLE LIKE TO DRAW WHAT THEY SEE AND WRITE WHAT THEY FEEL, OR YOU COULD JUST DO NOTHING AND LET YOUR MIND RELAX.*

TASMAN
NATIONAL PARK

Wild and exciting, beautiful and rugged all at the same time. Be prepared to have your breath taken away at Tasman National Park. Cliffs that make boats look tiny and sea caves bigger than buildings teeter on the edges of this one-of-a-kind park. Come and visit to feel windswept and truly alive.

TASMAN NATIONAL PARK

ID CARD

PARK ESTABLISHED: 1999
KNOWN FOR: SEA CAVES, WILD BUSHLAND AND OCEAN TEEMING WITH AQUATIC ANIMALS
SIZE: 107KM^2
HOME OF: PAYTIRAMI PEOPLE
GEOGRAPHY: GIANT TOWERS OF ROCK SOAR ABOVE THE RAGING OCEAN

SWIFT PARROT

Chit Chit... it's a Swift Parrot zooming through the sky at breakneck speed. One individual was even recorded flying at 88km per hour. See them hanging upside-down to get the best Blue Gum nectar – they're unmistakable with a long purple tail, a splash of red and a swish of blue. These parrots are migratory, staying in Tasmania for the breeding season and flying to the mainland for winter. Unfortunately they're Critically Endangered because so much of their habitat has been cut down.

FORTY-SPOTTED PARDALOTE

Tiny eyes watch you carefully as you walk past the Manna Gum upon which these teeny-weeny birds completely rely. This pardalote is found only in Tasmania and is now a threatened species. Of course they eat insects and larvae like most birds, but also manna – a sweet sap found under the bark of these special gums. Manna gives the tiny birds big boosts of energy and was also traditionally used as medicine. Can you count twenty spots on each wing?

FUR SEALS

Moving lightning fast in the water and diving to depths of 200 metres to hunt for fish, squid and octopus; Australian and New Zealand Fur Seals call these chilly waters home. Spot them by their distinctive wiggly ears, a double layer of fur and adorable puppy-dog eyes. The males have darker fur around their neck that looks like a lion's mane. Watch and laugh as they slip, slide and galumph around on the rocky coastline.

CASTLES OF ROCK

Many thousands of years of the ocean and wind splashing and whipping against the cliffs of rocks have created beautiful shapes, patterns, tunnels and bridges. Whether you're visiting the ancient sea cave of Tasman's Arch, braving the 115 steps to Remarkable Cave, which is made of sandstone, or meandering along the wildlife-filled walk on the way to Maingon Blowhole, there's a true adventure around every corner.

TASMANIAN BLUE GUM

These magnificent trees are so important to the people of Tasmania that they've made them the state emblem. Many important species rely on this tree to survive because it provides food and safe habitat. In fact some animals, including the Swift Parrot, even travel all the way here from the mainland just to munch on the flowers as they bloom! Growing to 60m tall, these clever plants have evolved to be strong in the harsh conditions – they have a special powder on the outside that acts like sunscreen to protect them from extreme sun, while a wax on their leaves protects them from the cold.

COMMON DOLPHIN

This is a great spot to watch dolphin pods frolic. Scientists think that dolphins leap to communicate and perhaps different movements mean different things. Dolphins use **echolocation** to socialise and work in teams. They make a sound using their melon (the top of their head) and wait for it to echo back after bouncing off underwater objects.

BLOTCHED BLUE-TONGUE

Heavy bodies and little legs cause these curious skinks to lumber along ever so slowly. Catch them baking in the early morning sun to help get them moving for the day. Fabulous all-rounders, they have strong jaws for crunching down on snails and beetles, but also sometimes on more delicate foods such as flowers and berries. Did you know that instead of laying eggs like other **reptiles**, they have live babies just like humans do? After they're born, the young shed their skin and move out of home in just a few days. Incredible!

SOUTHERN BROWN BANDICOOT

Dig, dig, scratch, grunt – a bandicoot has found something yummy. At night you might spot these **nocturnal** nesters fossicking around for insects, worms and plants. You might even catch them running with a gallop like tiny little horses through the undergrowth. Bandicoots are very important for our **ecosystems** because they help to break down plant material and form new soil. They also spread nutrients and fungi across the forest to keep plants healthy and help them grow strong.

ACTIVITIES

FIND MY FOOD

Recheck your animal facts on the previous page to find out who eats what. Draw an arrow from the animal to the food it likes to eat and discover the complex food web of the Tasmanian bush.

"Unlike most rangers, we get to live in the national park. We walk out to our hut with a week's worth of food and then live there, helping the people walking the trails. That means that we get to see the park in all seasons."
Ranger Jessica

RANGER'S TIP

Watch where you put your feet in spring, and try to walk on the firm sand – nesting seabirds are about!

SALTY SEAL SNACKS

Draw on the dinner plate which foods a seal might like to eat. You might even like to write them a 'menu' for the day.

PERFECT POETRY *IN YOUR NOTEBOOK, WRITE AN ACROSTIC POEM ALL ABOUT BANDICOOTS.*

MOUNT FIELD
NATIONAL PARK

Ancient glaciers, rainforests and eucalypt forests have made this special place what it is today. Caves, artwork and tool-making sites tell us so much about the Aboriginal history here. Way up high in the clouds and snow, tread your path gently and tell stories as you go.

MOUNT FIELD NATIONAL PARK

ID CARD

PARK ESTABLISHED: 1916
KNOWN FOR: WORLD HERITAGE WILDERNESS, SKI FIELDS AND EPIC WATERFALLS
SIZE: 158.8KM^2
HOME OF: PALAWA PEOPLE (BIG RIVER NATION)
GEOGRAPHY: ALPINE LAKES REST QUIETLY ATOP MOUNTAINS SCATTERED WITH ANCIENT RAINFOREST AND SECRETIVE CREATURES

LITTLE EXPLORER'S GUIDE

TASMANIAN MOUNTAIN SHRIMP

Today, at Robert Tarn and other lakes, creeks and caves in this park where the glaciers once slid, thousands of shrimp can be found swimming. Almost unchanged for millions of years, these **crustaceans** show scientists what life could've been like long ago. New species are still being discovered and it's thought that learning to live in caves protected these critters from extreme outside temperatures as the weather changed. Some that still live in caves are blind because it's so dark they can't see anyway.

GLOW WORM

Like something from a dream, glow worms light up caves and rocky overhangs throughout the forest, turning it into a magical, twinkling extravaganza. These 'worms' are actually the **larvae** of ancient flies. They spend nine months in this form, living inside a sticky mucus tube and hanging off threads from the roof. At night, a chemical reaction happens inside their bodies and causes them to switch on their 'lights'. They mesmerise their **prey** with their twinkling, then trap them in the sticky lines and eat them up for dinner. Once the larvae are big enough, they rest inside their mucus tube that turns hard and out emerges an adult fly that looks a bit like a mosquito.

PINK ROBIN

You'll need your keenest senses in thick bush to spot a 'pinky'. Look for black and pink feathers on cute, round bodies and listen for their *chwit-tr-tr-tr-tr* calls. You might even be able to spot one of their plush comfy nests – made from squishy moss and tangled together with spider webs and soft leaves – perched dramatically on the end of a branch.

TASMANIAN FROGLET

Measuring just 3cm, these tiny froglets can only be found in mountain areas in Tasmania. After they've laid their eggs in water, they sink to protect them from **predators**. The froglets are difficult to spot; look for dark brown backs and bright red under the legs wherever there's water. In the warmer months they might trick you with a call that sounds like a lamb: *baaa-aa-aa*.

SNOW GUM

Leaves droop and sway in the breeze as the snow gums use the cold snow and frost to develop their beautiful colours. Eucalypts are called 'sclerophylls' – which means they have hard leaves – and can survive in harsh conditions. As they age, the trees get hit with wind, snow and ice, causing them to twist. Look for thick, strong, twisty trees on your visit – which one do you think is the oldest?

FANTASTIC FUNGI

Look down low and way up high – so many fungi to delight your eyes! Move slowly and focus on one spot for a while to let your eyes adjust to see different colours hidden among the green. Get up close and use a mirror to see the gills underneath, but never touch these beauties. Fungi come in all shapes and sizes and your best chance at spotting them is in wet areas or near creeks. Did you know that the bits you can see are just a small part of the fungi? Under the surface are thousands of kilometres of fungi networks helping the trees to grow and communicate with each other.

EASTERN BARRED BANDICOOT

Ecologists released bandicoots here to provide them a safe home away from foxes and humans as they were almost **extinct** in Victoria. They use special cameras to watch how they're doing and see them running and hiding in the tall grass; digging pits in loose soil looking for a yummy snack of plant bulbs, **invertebrates** and fruits.

PANDANI

Not found anywhere else on Earth, Pandani leaves are strong and droopy to help snow slide right off and protect the plant from cold winters. Their huge leaves (up to a metre long) and pink-and-white flowers can be seen in the summertime at Pandani Grove. Under the cover of night the bronzy wings of the Pandani Moth emerge from their slumber and eat nothing but these special plants.

TASMANIAN NATIVE-HEN

Affectionately named 'turbo chooks' by Tasmanians, these bold birds can't fly, but have super strong legs for running at turbo speed up to 50 km per hour – that's as fast as a car in the city! Hear them call *see-saw* as they wander about munching on bugs, worms and even tadpoles.

ACTIVITIES

VALUABLE VENN

Scientists compare and contrast often as it helps them learn more about the world around them. Use the Venn diagram to list animals from this chapter that eat only meat, eat only vegetation, or eat both.

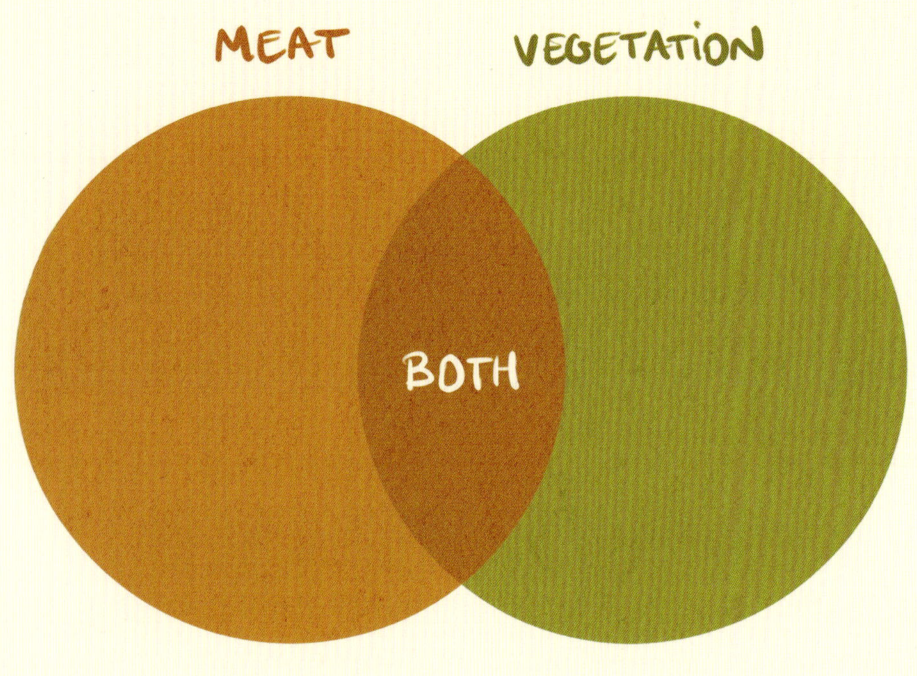

RANGER'S TIP

It can be fun to look at special things like fungi and glow worms from a different angle. Try getting down low and looking to the side or bending forward and viewing life upside-down.

"I love watching the change of seasons at Mount Field – the first snowfall of winter makes it look like a whole new world. I also love being the first one to leave my footprints in the snow!"
Ranger Brendan

PRETTY AS A PICTURE

Can you finish the picture of the Tasmanian Mountain Shrimp? Colour it in when you're done.

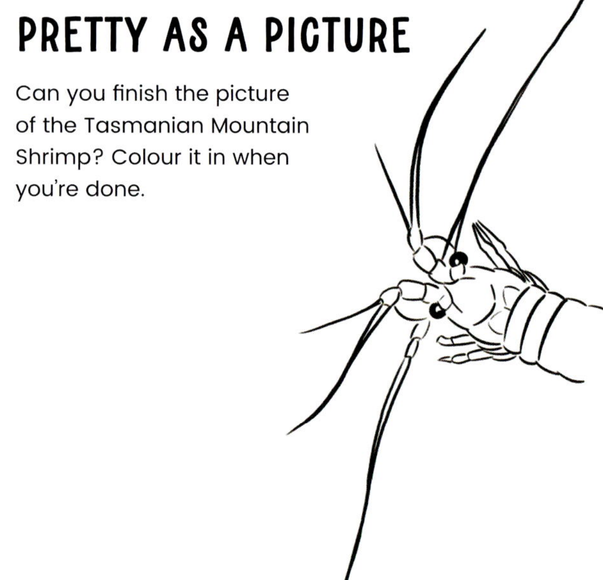

GET SET, GO

HOST A RUNNING RACE TO SEE WHO'S THE FASTEST TURBO CHOOK IN THE CAMPGROUND. EXTRA POINTS FOR MAKING ANIMAL SOUNDS AS YOU RUN.

FRANKLIN-GORDON *Wild Rivers* NATIONAL PARK

Deep in the forest, where birdsong floats on the breeze and the wind whispers through the trees, you'll find so many incredible sights. Huge rivers full of life and energy call to you, trees so tall you can't see the top tower over you and deep gorges make your jaw drop. Come camping, hiking, rafting and swimming for experiences you will never forget.

FRANKLIN-GORDON WILD RIVERS NATIONAL PARK

ID CARD

PARK ESTABLISHED: 1981
KNOWN FOR: THE FAMOUS FRANKLIN RIVER
SIZE: 4,400KM^2
HOME OF: PALAWA PEOPLE (SOUTH WEST AND BIG RIVER NATIONS)
GEOGRAPHY: DENSE ANCIENT RAINFOREST SCATTERED WITH CAVES AND ALIVE WITH TORRENTS OF FRESHWATER AROUND EACH NEW BEND

LITTLE EXPLORER'S GUIDE

TASMANIAN AZURE KINGFISHER

Plop! An Endangered kingfisher plummets into the water, fishing for insects, **crustaceans**, frogs and fish of course. Look for them in forest that hugs the rivers. Did you know that these birds use their strong beaks to dig holes along the riverbank to raise their babies? Inside are glossy, white eggs; bigger than the ones their cousins lay on the mainland.

EASTERN QUOLL

Hunting alone at night, quolls like to 'midnight feast' on birds, insects, **mammals** and **reptiles**. These **marsupial carnivores** are important for keeping pest numbers low because they also like a cheeky side dish of rabbits, mice and rats! You may see one dashing through the darkness – this species is cat-sized, brown-black and has no spots on its tail.

WHITE-BELLIED SEA-EAGLE

With a short, square tail and a distinctive honking call, these eagles are easy to spot. Their eyesight is twice as good as that of humans, with eyes further forward in their head (like binoculars) to allow them to zoom in really close. These birds can't break down all the parts of their **prey** in their bellies, so they regurgitate some as pellets and scientists use the information they contain in research.

SHORT-BEAKED ECHIDNA

Scratching around in the undergrowth, Echidnas use their long claws to tear open logs and nests so that they can spend hours snacking on ants, termites and worms. These spiny specimens use smell and special electrical signals in their snouts to find food. Watch out for them on the roads – these slow waddlers don't know how to cross!

THE FIGHT FOR THE FRANKLIN RIVER

In 1978, the Tasmanian Government tried to build a dam on the Franklin River to create hydroelectricity. Many people protested and five years later the dam was stopped. Renewable energy, such as creating electricity from water, does have benefits, but dams mean the river above the dam stops flowing and floods a wider area, while the river section below the dam gets a lot less water. Changing waterways affects how plants, animals and humans can live nearby. Some trees such as the Huon Pines are more than 3,000 years old and many rare and endangered animals live here too, not to mention the important Aboriginal sites that could've been lost.

KUTIKINA CAVE

Around 19,500 years ago, land connected Victoria and Tasmania and Aboriginal people walked across and began to live in this cave. That's a really long time ago – before humans arrived in America and before Egyptians lived along the Nile! In the 1970s, a scientist rafting down the river accidentally found the cave. The people who lived here long ago left behind important materials that help us understand history and there are more than 325,000 artefacts to learn from! Kutikina Cave has now been returned to its traditional owners who care for it.

NELSON FALLS

From a steady flow to a raging river, every day is different here. Take a wander through the ferns that are ancient descendants from **Gondwana** times and love the cool, wet climate here. Stand right above the water from the viewing platform and really listen. Can you see the rock wall that looks like steps, guiding each droplet down to the pool? At 30 metres high, this is a beautiful sight to see.

MACLEAY'S SWALLOWTAIL

Gently flapping their majestic black-and-green wings, edged with deep red and tipped with 'tails', these butterflies are easiest to find in the rainforest. Fat green caterpillars hatch from pale green eggs and crawl along leaves, sporting tiny white dots and a hump on their back. When they're nice and full, they make a chrysalis which cracks open around November. Look for male butterflies circling around the tops of 'their' trees – this is how they protect their territory.

ACTIVITIES

CODE CRACKER

Use the symbol alphabet below to uncover the secret sentence. Once you've solved this puzzle, have fun making your own!

_ _ _ _ _ _ _   _ _ _ _ _ _   _ _ _

_ _ _ _   _ _   _ _ _ _ _ _ _ _

WONDERFUL WATERFALL

Use your best addition skills to complete the number puzzle at Nelson Falls.

Clue: Each number is equal to the sum of the two boxes below it.

RANGER'S TIP

Drive along the Lyell Highway for easy access to short but beautiful hikes – perfect for little explorer legs!

"My favourite part of the job is walking through the incredible nature and the feeling of being absorbed by it. There are so many special experiences I've had here."

Ranger Frank

STORYTIME

PASSING DOWN STORIES FROM GENERATION TO GENERATION IS AN IMPORTANT WAY FOR CULTURES AROUND THE WORLD TO MAINTAIN TRADITIONS AND REMEMBER THEIR HISTORY. THINK ABOUT THE THINGS YOU HAVE SEEN OR DONE TODAY AND THINK UP YOUR OWN STORY TO TELL YOUR FAMILY AT BEDTIME TONIGHT.

Walls of Jerusalem NATIONAL PARK

Enormous walls of rock hug rolling valleys teeming with creatures. Squish-squash through marshy flats, crinch-crunch amid grassy plains and pop-hop over rocky boulders. Come and see all the weird and wonderful things that live in this fun park.

WALLS OF JERUSALEM NATIONAL PARK

ID CARD

PARK ESTABLISHED:	1981
KNOWN FOR:	INCREDIBLE HIKES THROUGH ALPINE FORESTS, LAKES AND STREAMS
SIZE:	518KM^2
HOME OF:	PALAWA PEOPLE (BIG RIVER NATION)
GEOGRAPHY:	TOWERING WALLS OF ROCK FLANK BEAUTIFUL VALLEYS WHERE GLACIERS ONCE DRIFTED

PENCIL PINE

Taking it nice and slow, pencil pines can live to over 1,200 years old! These incredible plants can literally clone themselves using suckers, so small groups are identical. Look closely – can you see how the leaves go around in spiral shapes? They're so close together that they look like scales. Look for the wrinkliest faces in the bark to discover which trees are the oldest.

GEOLOGICAL WONDER

Are you wondering how these huge walls made of a special rock called dolerite got here? Under the surface there are fault lines where the plates of the Earth meet. Each time they wiggle or bump together, the rock on top can move. The walls make lovely areas that are protected from the weather, where grasses and pine trees can grow, and even Aboriginal artefacts have been found inside the walls. Visit in the spring to see the scoparia bloom here in bright colours of pink, orange, gold and white.

BROWN TREE FROG

You've got a great chance of seeing the most common frog in the state near all these freshwater pools! These tiny brown **amphibians** call out *ree-ree-ree-ree-ree-ree* after rain. They love to climb, and to do so they use special discs on their toes and fingers for grabbing on tight. Up to 700 sticky eggs are laid at once, that cling to the undersides of water plants.

METALLIC SKINK

As the climate changes, Metallic Skinks are moving into new territories, taking over **habitat** of other lizards. Look for a metallic shine and pink-orange belly hidden beneath leaves, rocks and logs. These skinks don't lay eggs – instead they give birth to live babies like humans. Another trick is that they can regrow their own tail.

LONG-TAILED MOUSE

Beautiful, perfectly round eyes belong to a special shy creature that lives only in Tasmania. *Boing!* Very long back feet help them to leap over rocks and long tails likely assist with balance. These rodents look especially cute when they push their furry round ears forward to cover their eyes. Did you know that scientists can tell how old an animal is by how ground down its teeth are?

LOWLANDS COPPERHEAD

Muscly, scaly bodies slither through the undergrowth looking for their next meal of **ectothermic prey**, such as a frog, lizard or even another snake. Copperheads are especially clever because they give birth to live young instead of laying eggs and can live in cold places where most snakes can't survive. Scared snakes will hiss and throw their bodies around and, although they prefer not to bite, are dangerously **venomous**.

GREY BUTCHERBIRD

Some say that this bird's song is the most beautiful in the bush. Bold and cheeky with humans, butcherbirds get their name because of the way they hang their **prey** up in the trees – they even have a hook on their beak to help them. Baby butcherbirds snuggle into comfy nests lined with grass, and once they've 'left home' they often stay around the neighbourhood to help their parents look after their new younger brothers and sisters.

GALAXIIDS

Fish with no scales? Is this magic? More than 60 per cent of fish found in freshwater habitats of Tasmania are galaxiids. They lay hundreds of eggs at a time that stick to rocks along the shore where mums and dads watch over them until they're born. Sit and watch patiently. How many can you count?

ACTIVITIES

NEW SPECIES ALERT!

Invent your own new creature by combining the top and bottom halves of two that live here. Which special skills will it have and what will its name be?

RANGER'S TIP

Wild animals such as butcherbirds may be cheeky and particularly friendly but human food can make them sick, so it's not a good idea to share your food with them.

"The Walls of Jerusalem National Park is a very spiritual place for me. There is so much more to see than just the views from the mountain tops. There are worlds within worlds up here."
Ranger Chris

COMPASS ADVENTURE

Help the galaxiids swim their way around the streams to a safe place to lay their eggs. Follow the arrows to find out which nesting ground they like best.

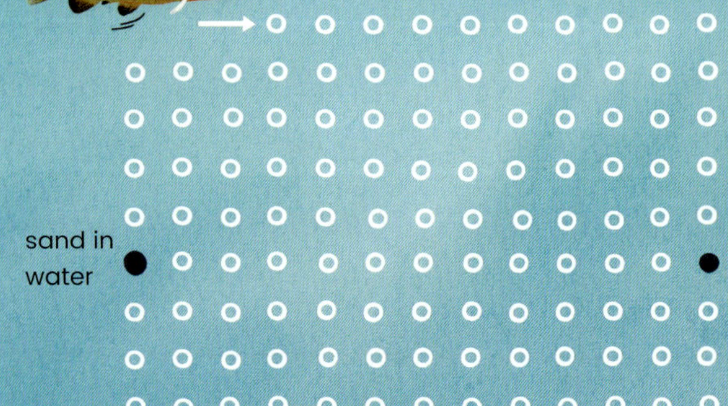

SHADOW SHOW *USE A TORCH AT NIGHT TO MAKE SHADOWS WITH YOUR HANDS OR CARDBOARD FROM YOUR RECYCLING AND TELL A STORY ABOUT THE ANIMALS THAT CALL THIS ANCIENT PLACE HOME.*

SOUTHWEST NATIONAL PARK

Among forests that are famous the world over, come and find truly ancient trees, endangered birds and hilarious creatures of the night. The biggest park in Tasmania will take you everywhere from lakes to mountains, beaches and grassy plains. Explorers can expect fantastic walks and the excitement of weather that changes super quickly just to keep you on your toes.

SOUTHWEST NATIONAL PARK

ID CARD

PARK ESTABLISHED: 1968
KNOWN FOR: WORLD HERITAGE FORESTS
SIZE: 6,183KM^2
HOME OF: PALAWA PEOPLE (SOUTH WEST NATION)
GEOGRAPHY: JAGGED MOUNTAINS SPLIT BY SWEEPING VALLEYS

HUON PINE

Can you feel that breeze in your hair? That's the same wind that tickles the branches of the Huon Pines and causes clouds of pollen to puff right out of the cones and get carried away to make new plants. Many people use Huon timber to build boats and houses because it has a special oil that stops it from rotting and protects against pests. Perhaps the most special thing about these trees is their age. Their ancestors were growing when dinosaurs walked the Earth and in Tasmania conditions are perfect for each tree to live until it is 3,000 years old. Incredible!

GREEN ROSELLA

These strong flyers are found all across Tasmania but nowhere on the mainland. They look pretty funny when they hold food in their feet to eat and call *cussik cussik* to their friends. Look up for tree hollows where they build their nests, you might even catch one chewing around the entrance to make it bigger to squeeze inside.

SHORT-TAILED SHEARWATER

Also called 'mutton birds', these hilarious feathered friends make for funny birdwatching. Their bodies are so perfectly designed to soar above the ocean that coming in to land is particularly tricky for them – so you might catch them crashing into trees, bushes or buildings as they make their clumsy descent. There are more than 200 shearwater colonies here, making more than 11 MILLION burrows across Tasmania. Each burrow contains a single egg or chick.

MOSS FROGLET

Tick-tok-tok-tok-tok, did someone drop a ping-pong ball? Nope, it's just a tiny Moss Froglet calling to its mates. This incredible specimen isn't your ordinary **amphibian**. It lays its eggs in lichen in the rainforest and then the tadpoles grow on land instead of in water. Isn't that amazing?

ORANGE-BELLIED PARROT

As the weather cools during the autumn months, these extremely rare parrots fly north to the mainland, not returning again until the warmer days of spring when they come home to raise new broods of young. They usually wait until there's a strong wind that can push them along and make the journey quicker. These magnificent birds are Critically Endangered and scientists are using leg bands to track their movements and providing artificial nestboxes for their young. I wonder if you can spot them feeding on the buttongrass or calling *zit-zit-zit* when they're alarmed.

COMMON BRUSH-TAILED POSSUM

Resting in tree hollows during the day and dashing out at night for some **nocturnal** fun, 'brushies' might cause a commotion at your campsite as they bang, crash and scamper over human items. Their brush tail, cute pink nose and confident attitude makes them pretty likeable. They love eating leaves, flowers and fruits all night long.

BUTTONGRASS PLAINS

The way the buttongrass catches the light just right makes every photo look like a postcard. Growing in clumps on the ground, this plant is an important hiding place for rare birds and **mammals**. Stay on the tracks to keep it healthy.

FRESHWATER BURROWING CRAYFISH

As you trudge around the wet areas, look out for mud stacks (some as tall as a school ruler) at tunnel entrances in the riverbanks. These are the elaborate homes of crayfish and scientists still don't know why they do this. What do you think? These clever **crustaceans** are perfectly adapted to their lifestyle and have developed claws that open up and down (vertically) so they can fit into their tight tunnels. See them chomping on rotting leaves and sticks – an important part of the forest cycle.

ACTIVITIES

LIFECYCLE FUN

Order the pictures of the Moss Froglet to show the stages of its metamorphic lifecycle.

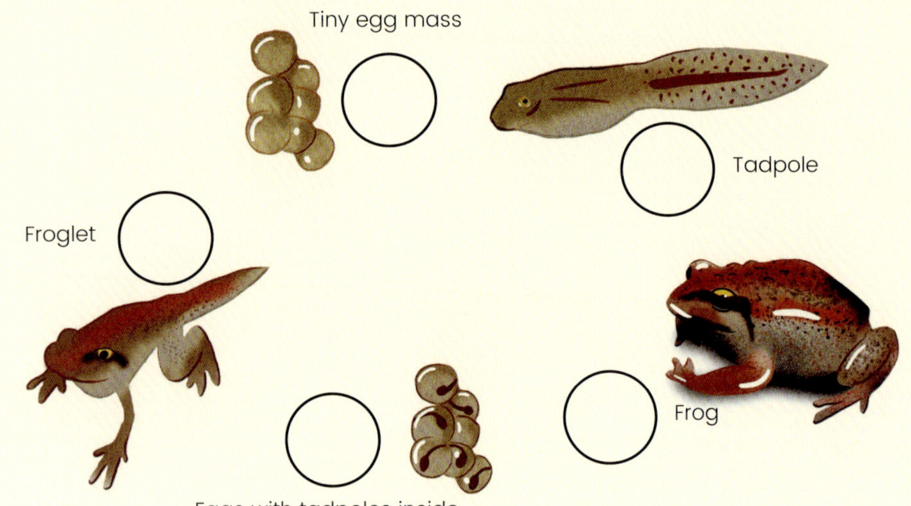

"I love being out in the middle of the wilderness away from civilisation, watching the changing light and weather and experiencing nature at its best."
Ranger Dave

RANGER'S TIP

Some plants such as buttongrass are easily affected by diseases that are carried from other places. Clean your boots, explorers!

PRETTY AS A PARROT

Colour the Orange-bellied Parrot according to the numbers in each box, then marvel at your gorgeous artwork.

 1

 2

 3

 4

 5

NATURE PORTRAIT

USE NATURAL MATERIALS AROUND YOUR CAMPGROUND TO DESIGN A PICTURE OF A HUGE HUON PINE IN THE SOIL. PUT THE ITEMS BACK WHERE YOU FOUND THEM WHEN YOU'VE FINISHED PLAYING.

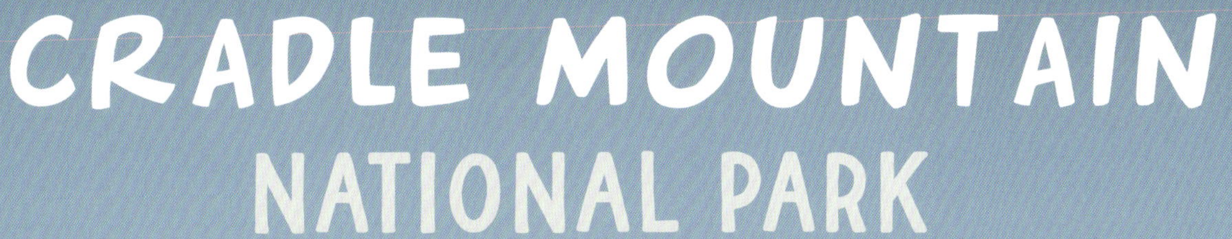

CRADLE MOUNTAIN NATIONAL PARK

The marvels in this World Heritage area are seriously ancient. Animals and plants here are resilient and strong, just like the mountain upon which they live. There are walks to suit everyone's abilities. With a view that changes around every corner, over every peak and reinvents itself with each season, it's no wonder this park is so special to the ancestors of this land.

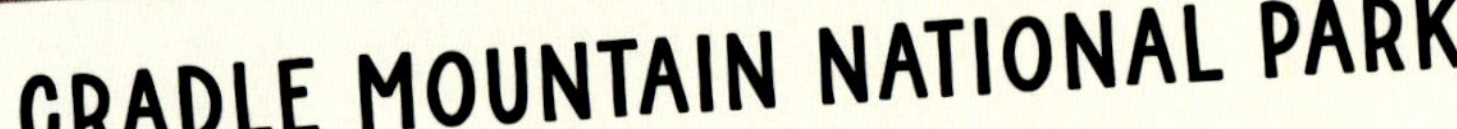

CRADLE MOUNTAIN NATIONAL PARK

ID CARD

PARK ESTABLISHED:	1922
KNOWN FOR:	CRADLE MOUNTAIN AND WOMBATS IN THE SNOW
SIZE:	1,614KM^2
HOME OF:	LARMAIRREMENER AND WEEBONENETINER PEOPLE
GEOGRAPHY:	DEEP FRESHWATER LAKES SLEEPING BELOW COLD MOUNTAIN TOPS

CUSHION PLANTS

An illusion to behold, a cushion plant is actually a whole group of plants that grow slowly and all together in clumps, to protect each other from the cold and wind – what teamwork! They're pretty fragile, so cheer them on by sticking to the paths and walking around (not on top) when you spot them.

BARE-NOSED WOMBAT

Strong, robust and furry, these lovely waddling creatures make the perfect mountaineers. At sunset, wombats shuffle about to feed on whatever is available – leaves, grass, bark, moss and even fungi. Did you know that wombats use their strong claws for digging huge burrows 20 metres long and 2 metres deep? Even their pouches face backwards so that the babies don't get a face full of dirt! Each wombat marks its territory with scent by rubbing up against things – logs and rocks will look 'polished' from so much rubbing. These weird and wonderful creatures have super elastic intestines that create cube-shaped poo that won't roll off the side of the mountain. Poo also marks territory, so these wombats like to arrange their cubes in a stack – the higher the better.

THYLACINE

Gone but not forgotten, the Thylacine hasn't been seen alive since the 1930s and is now **extinct**. Very slow and steady, these semi-**nocturnal** dog-shaped beauties would feast on kangaroos using their 46 sharp teeth to devour them. Humans began to hunt Thylacines when they believed they were eating farm animals and sadly it was too little too late when the species finally became protected only two months after the last one died in a zoo. The Thylacine is our reminder to respect the purpose of every species in its natural area and to learn to live alongside each other.

MOUNTAIN DRAGON

Scurry, scurry, stop! Mountain Dragons use 'crypsis' to confuse **predators**; they run away then freeze, camouflaging perfectly into the leaf litter. **Predators** expect them to keep running, so their eye moves past the lizard, which makes it almost impossible to find again. Unlike other lizards these fellows can live in super-cold places because they go into 'torpor' for seven months, which is a bit like hibernating to save energy and escape the cold.

PLATYPUS

Shhhh... Platypuses have amazing hearing. As you peer into the dark, cool water, past your own reflection, watch carefully for bubbles floating to the surface. Platypuses use special sensors in their bills to track the electrical signals of their **prey** underwater. They forage and sift for **invertebrates** at the bottom, which makes the bubbles you can see, and then stash the food in their cheeks to grind up later. These monotremes are **mammals**, but also lay two eggs! Mums don't have a pouch, so they snuggle their babies in the burrow instead.

FAGUS

The Fagus is the only tree that loses its leaves here. In autumn, their leaves that look like crinkle cut chips turn and splash colours of gold, red and orange across the landscape before they fall off and leave magical twisted grey branches exposed for the winter.

AURORA AUSTRALIS

Way up in the sky, particles in the sun build up charge, then explode out into space, creating a solar wind. The wind gets pulled towards the South Pole and the tiny particles around it hit the gases in the Earth's atmosphere and make ribbons of colour across the sky. The best time to see our auroras is on cloudless nights when the moon is in a new or crescent phase, so its light doesn't spoil the view.

PENCIL PINE MOTH

Only in Tasmania will you find this moth high up where the Pencil Pines live. Recently many pines were lost to fire, which has impacted moth families because their only food source is the Pencil Pine. You'll have to use keen senses to spot the red-brown caterpillars with skin so thick it looks like it's made of scales, because they are so perfectly **camouflaged** in the tree. After **metamorphosis**, beautiful moths are revealed boasting black and grey wing patterns and a dash of orange surprise when they open to fly away.

TASMANIAN DEVIL

The largest **carnivorous marsupial** in the world is Endangered and lives right here, resting during the day in dens of hollow logs, rocks and caves. At night these noisy eaters emerge to hunt, eating all parts of their catch, even the bones and fur! They use strong teeth and powerful jaws to tear **marsupials**, **mammals**, birds, **reptiles**, **amphibians** and insects apart. Sometimes they open their mouths wide and make fierce monster noises, which is how they got the name 'devil'.

ACTIVITIES

SPOT THE DIFFERENCE

Compare the two drawings of the Pencil Pine Moth and circle the six differences.

RANGER'S TIP

Weather conditions in alpine environments are very changeable. Check the weather forecast before you go and carry appropriate gear for every season.

"Cradle Mountain's beauty and its resilience under harsh winter conditions is inspiring."
Ranger Taylor

COMMON GROUND

Which of these animals have something in common? Do you know what it is?

COOL CAMO *JUST LIKE A PENCIL PINE MOTH, DRESS YOURSELF UP IN COLOURS THAT OFFER CAMOUFLAGE AGAINST THE BACKGROUND OF THE FOREST AROUND YOU. PLAY HIDE-AND-SEEK WITH YOUR TRAVEL COMPANIONS AND SEE WHO CAN STAY HIDDEN THE LONGEST. REMEMBER TO ALWAYS TELL YOUR ADULTS WHERE YOU ARE BEFORE YOU START PLAY.*

South Bruny
NATIONAL PARK

Only a short ferry trip away, South Bruny is suited to the whole family. Swim at sheltered beaches where crisp cool waves lap gently at the shore, head out with binoculars to discover the hundreds of birds that surround you and take long walks on the beach as you relax in this beautiful landscape.

SOUTH BRUNY NATIONAL PARK

ID CARD

LITTLE EXPLORER'S GUIDE

PARK ESTABLISHED:	1997
KNOWN FOR:	AMAZING SCENERY
SIZE:	5,000KM^2
HOME OF:	NUNUNI PEOPLE OF LUNAWUNI (BRUNY ISLAND)
GEOGRAPHY:	A HEART OF RAINFOREST ENCIRCLED BY ROCKY COASTLINE

BLACK PEPPERMINT TREE

Where the soil is sandy, feel the rough bark of the peppermint trees as you pass on by. For a full sensory experience sniff the leaves – can you smell peppermint? Traditionally these leaves and gum were used to make medicine, the bark to make everyday materials and the seeds eaten. Did you know that these trees grow a 'lignotuber'? It's a special part that stays underground and helps the plant regrow if the top is cut or damaged by fire. Incredible!

LEOPARD SEAL

Usually living in Antarctica, Leopard Seals stop for a rest in Tasmania every once in a while. Expert ocean hunters, their favourite thing to eat is tiny krill and they even have special teeth that work like a sieve to let water rush out and trap krill inside. Watch out for splashing in the water, sometimes they throw their **prey** (such as birds) around before eating it! Can you guess how they got their name?

MUDFLATS

Incredible **habitat** for plants and animals, many migratory birds live and feed on the mudflats you see here. That's not all – did you know that **sediment** runs off the land, down the river and sinks to the bottom of these flats? This process leaves the clear water to run out to sea. Special bacteria live in the mud and break down any organic matter including branches and leaves. This releases important nutrients and helps plants to grow, completing the circle of life.

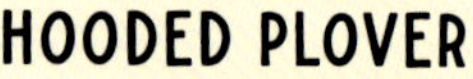

HOODED PLOVER

Pecking at the edges where the water licks the sand are sweet little Endangered plovers, hungry for miniscule marine creatures. Watch them run quickly on tiny legs, zigzagging this way and that. When it's time to lay eggs, they scrape out some sand and plonk them right in a hollow on the ground. About half of all the east-coast Hooded Plovers live in Tasmania, making it extra important to protect this **habitat**.

CAPE BRUNY LIGHTHOUSE

Peek inside for a look back in time to 1836 when this incredible structure was built. In the days when lighthouse lamps were powered by whale oil, this beauty helped to guide many ships safely to shore. Early convicts built the lighthouse you see today Imagine what hard work it must have been to make a structure that's more than 100 metres tall.

HUMPBACK WHALE

Humpbacks sing their dreamy songs in these waters and have made a huge comeback from the brink of extinction in the 1960s. These big grey babies grow up to 16 metres long! That's about the same length as 84 pencils or 4.5 small cars! The whales love to show off as they travel the coastline – don't forget to wave back.

WHITE WALLABY

The famous and very cute white wallabies of Tasmania are so used to being snapped by the human paparazzi that they've become pretty friendly – look but don't touch. These are actually Bennett's Wallabies that have been separated from mainland populations for so long they are genetically different. Their colouring is called 'albino' and it's pretty easy to spot them at sunset and sunrise with their white fur and pink eyes and nose.

LITTLE PYGMY POSSUM

Nectar, pollen, insects and spiders are such yummy treats for pygmy possums that they spend their lives following food – wherever the flowers are is where you'll find them. Look about in branches close to the ground for their tiny pink noses and long whiskers – it's harder to get eaten by nocturnal birds of prey if you stay down low and go, go, go. Big eyes let in more light and help them to see at night, while special adaptations mean they can force themselves into a big rest (torpor) if the weather gets too cold for their little bodies.

ACTIVITIES

NATURE SUDOKU

Complete the sudoku puzzle by drawing in the missing icons. Each image must appear only once in each row, column and grid.

"I love wandering through coastal heath on the Labillardiere Peninsula when the spring wildflowers are in bloom, and visiting Cloudy Bay during the wild winter storms."
Ranger Nick

RANGER'S TIP

Whales can be tricky to spot way out in the ocean. Pack a pair of binoculars for your adventures or hold your eyes steady, focusing on one area for ten seconds to check for movement.

DEEP INTO DRAWING

Have a go at drawing your own pygmy possum using the steps below.

SKETCHES IN THE SAND

TAKE SOME TIME TO SLOW IT DOWN AND DESIGN A MANDALA IN THE SAND. NOTICE HOW CALM YOU FEEL BY THE TIME YOU FINISH.

FINAL QUIZ

Now that you've finished your reading and exploring, here's one last quiz to check what you learned. Check back through the book for the answers.

1. What is the second-largest marsupial in the world?

2. Why is kelp so important?

3. What helps banksia cones to open and release seed?

4. How fast can 'turbo chooks' run?

5. Why do Pandani have strong, droopy leaves?

6. Where can you find mountain shrimps?

7. What shape is wombat poo?

8. What are three types of ectothermic prey that copperhead snakes like to eat?

9. What do echidnas use their long claws for?

10. What do blue-tongues like to do in the early morning?

Answers on inside back cover.

KEYWORDS EXPLAINED

Amphibian Cold-blooded animals with a backbone that can breathe underwater at a stage of their life.

Camouflage When animals and plants match their colours to their surroundings to blend in and hide from predators.

Carnivore Eats only meat.

Crustacean Animals that usually live in water and have a hard shell, segmented body and joints.

Diurnal Animals that are active during the day.

Ecologist A scientist who studies animals, plants, air and water.

Ecosystem A community of living things in their natural environment.

Echolocation The skill many animals use to find objects using sounds reflected back to them.

Erosion When soil, rock or sand is slowly worn away by wind or water.

Extinct When all the animals and plants of a particular species have died out.

Fauna Animals.

Flora Plants.

Gondwanaland A huge mass of land millions of years ago that was made up of many of today's continents before they broke apart.

Habitat The place where animals and plants live and gain everything they require to survive.

Herbivore Eats only plant matter.

Hibernate When animals rest for long periods without eating or reproducing.

Incubate When animals keep their eggs warm to help the babies develop and hatch.

Invertebrate Animal without a backbone.

Mammal Warm-blooded animals that produce milk.

Marsupial Mammals that have pouches.

Migrate When animals temporarily move from one area to another in search of food, a mate or better weather.

Nocturnal Animals that sleep during the day and hunt or forage at night.

Omnivore Eats both meat and plant matter

Predator An animal or plant that eats other animals or plants.

Prey An animal or plant that gets eaten by other animals or plants.

Reptile Cold-blooded animals with a backbone that have scaly skin.

Scat Animal poo

Sediment Tiny particles of soil in water that eventually settle to the bottom.

Venomous An animal that injects or secretes a dangerous substance into its prey or animals that pose a threat.

PLEDGE TO THE PLANET

Now you know all about Tasmanian National Parks and how to make better choices to protect plants, animals and culture; you can show your commitment by saying the pledge.

Have an adult record you speaking the pledge and signing it.

As a child of the world and a responsible citizen of our community,
I pledge to do what I can at home, at school and in my community,
To use less stuff,
Find new ways to do things,
Get outside more often,
Keep my distance from wild animals,
Respect and celebrate the culture of the places I visit,
Tell people about the amazing things I've learnt about nature; and
Do the right thing even when nobody is looking.
I love my planet and we can all work together to keep it healthy for our future.

Signed . . . .

FIND OUT MORE

For keen little scientists wanting to read more about the fascinating animals, plants and culture detailed in this book, you can read on here:

Australian Geographic
Australian Marine Conservation Society
Australian Museum
Australians Together
BirdLife Australia
Bush Heritage Australia
Fungimap
Marine Conservation Institute
The Nature Conservancy
Tasmanian Parks and Wildlife Service
United Nations Educational, Scientific and Cultural Organisation (UNESCO)
Wildlife Information Rescue and Education Service (WIRES)
World Wildlife Fund (WWF)

Published in 2026 by Reed New Holland Publishers
newhollandpublishers.com

A record of this book is held at the National Library of Australia.
ISBN 9781760796877
Managing Director: Fiona Schultz
General Manager: Olga Dementiev
Publisher and Project Editor: Simon Papps
Designer: Andrew Davies
Production Director: Arlene Gippert

OTHER TITLES BY REED NEW HOLLAND INCLUDE:

Little Explorer's Guide to Australian National Parks ISBN 9781760796150
Little Explorer's Guide to New South Wales National Parks ISBN 9781921073151
Little Explorer's Guide to Queensland National Parks ISBN 9781760795214
Little Explorer's Guide to Victorian National Parks ISBN 9781760796167
Chris Humfrey's Awesome Australian Animals ISBN 9781925546705
Chris Humfrey's Coolest Creepy Crawlies ISBN 9781760794453
Chris Humfrey's Incredible Coastal Critters ISBN 9781760794460

For details of hundreds of other Natural History titles see newhollandpublishers.com

And keep up with Reed New Holland and New Holland Publishers on Facebook and Instagram
ReedNewHolland and NewHollandPublishers
@ReedNewHolland and @NewHollandPublishers